U.S.A. TRAVEL GUIDES

ARIZONA

BY ANN HEINRICHS • ILLUSTRATED BY MATT KANIA

The Child's World®
childsworld.com

Published by The Child's World®
1980 Lookout Drive • Mankato, MN 56003-1705
800-599-READ • www.childsworld.com

ISBN 9781503819436
LCCN 2016961120

Printing
Printed in the United States of America
PA02334

About the Author
Ann Heinrichs

Ann Heinrichs is the author of more than 100 books for children and young adults. She has also enjoyed successful careers as a children's book editor and an advertising copywriter. Ann grew up in Fort Smith, Arkansas, and lives in Chicago, Illinois.

About the
Map Illustrator
Matt Kania

Matt Kania loves maps and, as a kid, dreamed of making them. In school he studied geography and cartography, and today he makes maps for a living. Matt's favorite thing about drawing maps is learning about the places they represent. Many of the maps he has created can be found in books, magazines, videos, Web sites, and public places.

On the cover: The Grand Canyon is the most iconic landmark in Arizona.

OUR ARIZONA TRIP

ARIZONA

Shall we tour Arizona today? It's a wonderland of things to see and do! Just wait and learn what's in store.

You'll ride a mule into the Grand Canyon. You'll hike through the desert and pan for gold. You'll pick pumpkins and pet potbellied pigs. You'll meet gunfighters and rattlesnakes. And you'll stay up late for stargazing!

That's a lot of stuff for one state! So saddle up and buckle yourself in. It's time to hit the road!

WELCOME TO ARIZONA

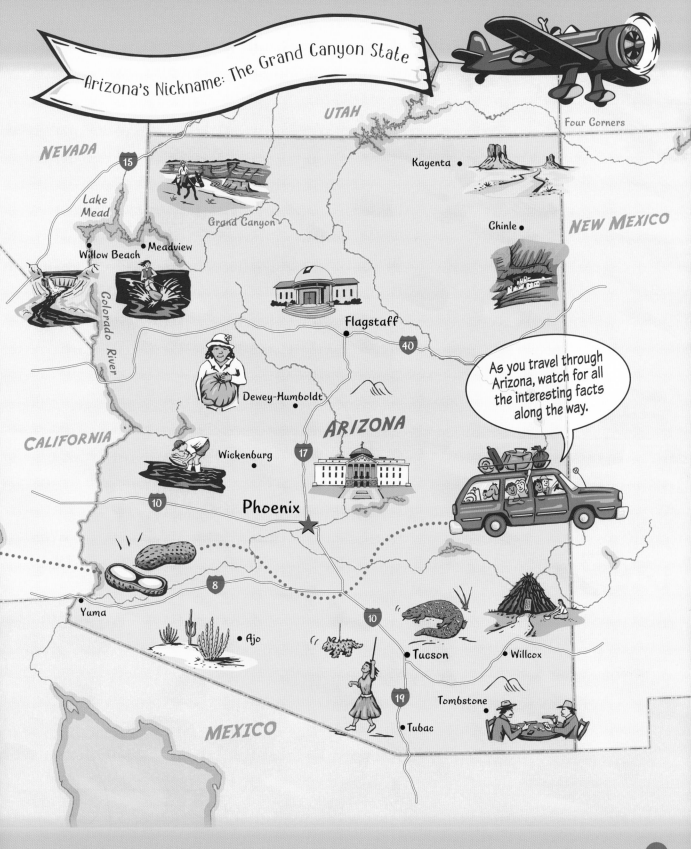

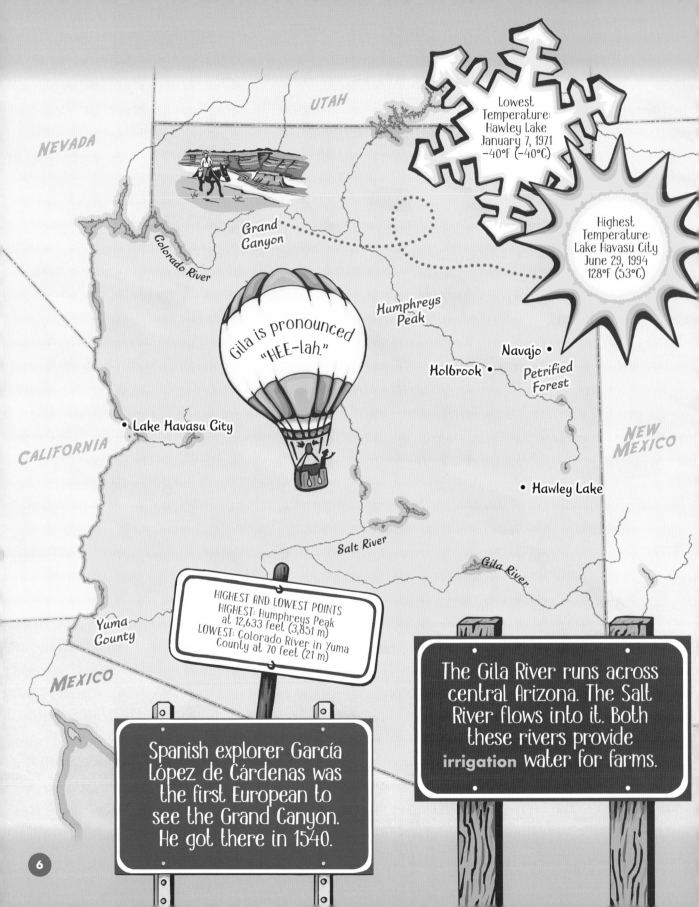

NEVADA

UTAH

Lowest Temperature:
Hawley Lake
January 7, 1971
−40°F (−40°C)

Highest Temperature:
Lake Havasu City
June 29, 1994
128°F (53°C)

Colorado River

Grand Canyon

Gila is pronounced "HEE-lah."

Humphreys Peak

Navajo •
Holbrook •   Petrified Forest

• Lake Havasu City

CALIFORNIA

NEW MEXICO

• Hawley Lake

Salt River

Gila River

Yuma County

MEXICO

HIGHEST AND LOWEST POINTS
HIGHEST: Humphreys Peak
at 12,633 feet (3,851 m)
LOWEST: Colorado River in Yuma
County at 70 feet (21 m)

The Gila River runs across central Arizona. The Salt River flows into it. Both these rivers provide **irrigation** water for farms.

Spanish explorer García López de Cárdenas was the first European to see the Grand Canyon. He got there in 1540.

THE GRAND CANYON

Saddle up your mule. Then hop on for a long trail ride. He's taking you down into the Grand Canyon! It's Arizona's most famous natural site. The canyon's colorful rock walls are awesome.

The Colorado River wore away this deep **gorge**. The river cuts across northwestern Arizona. Then it forms most of Arizona's western border.

Highlands cover much of northern Arizona. This region has many mountains and high **plateaus**. Rivers have carved interesting rock formations there. Land in southern Arizona is more low lying. Deserts cover much of this area. But the south has some mountain ranges, too.

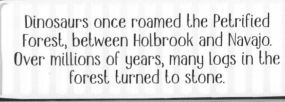

Dinosaurs once roamed the Petrified Forest, between Holbrook and Navajo. Over millions of years, many logs in the forest turned to stone.

Boat down the Colorado River. The canyon rises high on both sides of the river!

MONUMENT VALLEY AND FOUR CORNERS

Have you ever seen a butte? (Butte rhymes with cute!) It's a rocky hill with steep sides and a flat top. Just visit Monument Valley, north of Kayenta. You'll see buttes galore!

Two famous buttes are named the Mitten Buttes. They look like a pair of mittens! Another pair is called the Bear and Rabbit. Other buttes are named Elephant Butte and Gray Whiskers.

Next, travel east to the Four Corners. You'll want to stand in this famous spot. The borders of four states come together there. Which states? Arizona, Colorado, New Mexico, and Utah. You can touch all four at the same time!

The West Mitten Butte (left) and East Mitten Butte (right) are icons of the American West.

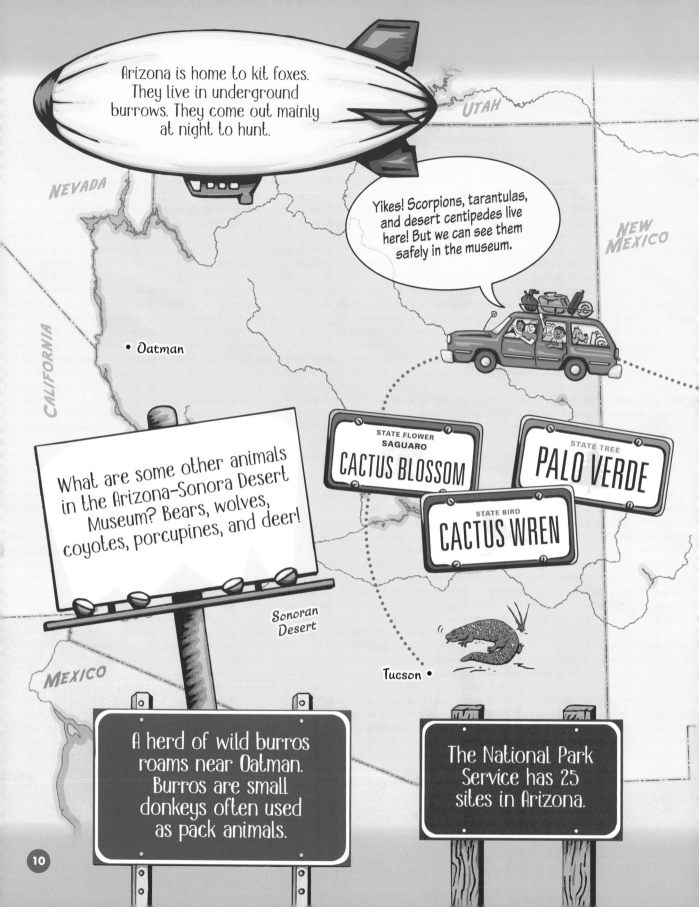

Arizona is home to kit foxes. They live in underground burrows. They come out mainly at night to hunt.

UTAH

NEVADA

Yikes! Scorpions, tarantulas, and desert centipedes live here! But we can see them safely in the museum.

NEW MEXICO

• Oatman

CALIFORNIA

What are some other animals in the Arizona-Sonora Desert Museum? Bears, wolves, coyotes, porcupines, and deer!

STATE FLOWER
SAGUARO
CACTUS BLOSSOM

STATE TREE
PALO VERDE

STATE BIRD
CACTUS WREN

Sonoran Desert

Tucson •

MEXICO

A herd of wild burros roams near Oatman. Burros are small donkeys often used as pack animals.

The National Park Service has 25 sites in Arizona.

Wander along the winding trail. Suddenly, you're face-to-face with a mountain lion!

Don't freak out. There's a glass wall between you. You're visiting the Arizona-Sonora Desert Museum! It's in the Sonoran Desert near Tucson. There you'll meet desert animals in their natural surroundings.

You'll see how a rattlesnake's tail works. Prairie dogs will peek out from their burrows. And hummingbirds might even whiz by you.

All these animals live in the Sonoran Desert. So do geckos, horned lizards, and iguanas. But watch out for Gila monsters. They're large lizards with a poisonous bite!

This great horned owl calls the Arizona-Sonora Desert Museum home.

ORGAN PIPE CACTUS NATIONAL MONUMENT

How many types of cactus are there? Just visit Organ Pipe Cactus National Monument. It's south of Ajo on the Mexican border. You'll see 28 types of cactus there!

All kinds of cactus grow in Arizona. Some are saguaro (sah-WAH-ro), cholla (CHO-yah), prickly pear, and hedgehog cactus. Each one has a special shape and size. It's easy to spot the organ pipe cactus. Its tall arms branch out from the base.

Saguaro National Park is near Tucson. Giant saguaro cactus grow there. They often mature as tall as a four-story building. They look like people holding their arms up!

Most U.S. organ pipe cactus grow in Organ Pipe Cactus National Monument.

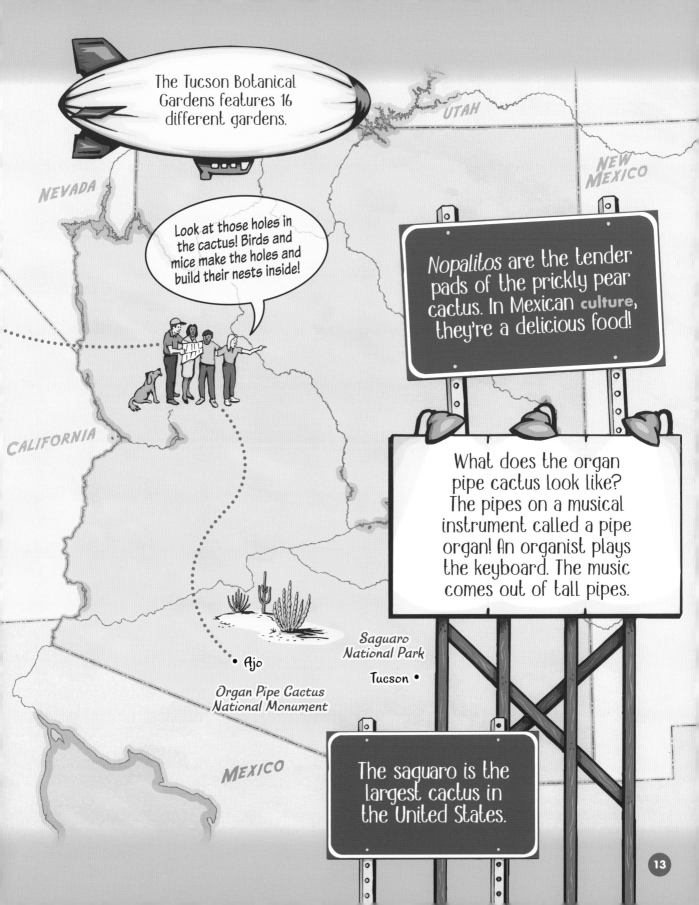

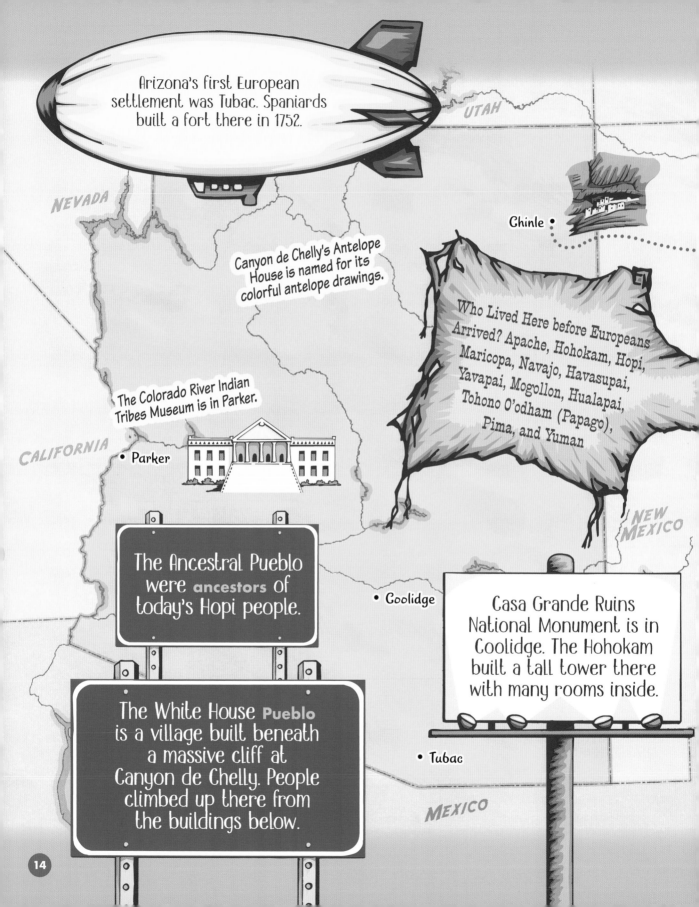

Arizona's first European settlement was Tubac. Spaniards built a fort there in 1752.

UTAH

NEVADA

Chinle •

Canyon de Chelly's Antelope House is named for its colorful antelope drawings.

Who Lived Here before Europeans Arrived? Apache, Hohokam, Hopi, Maricopa, Navajo, Havasupai, Yavapai, Mogollon, Hualapai, Tohono O'odham (Papago), Pima, and Yuman

The Colorado River Indian Tribes Museum is in Parker.

CALIFORNIA

• Parker

NEW MEXICO

The Ancestral Pueblo were **ancestors** of today's Hopi people.

• Coolidge

Casa Grande Ruins National Monument is in Coolidge. The Hohokam built a tall tower there with many rooms inside.

The White House **Pueblo** is a village built beneath a massive cliff at Canyon de Chelly. People climbed up there from the buildings below.

• Tubac

MEXICO

> Look at the White House Pueblo tucked into that cliff! That's amazing!

CANYON DE CHELLY

Don't miss Canyon de Chelly near Chinle. (Chelly is pronounced "SHAY.") You'll see homes high in the canyon walls. It's hard to imagine how they were built! They're ancient dwellings of the Ancestral Pueblo people. They lived here more than 1,000 years ago. Today, Navajo guides teach visitors about the history of the canyon.

The Hohokam lived in central Arizona. They built a massive irrigation system. It brought water to their crops. The Mogollon lived in eastern Arizona.

Spanish explorers arrived in the 1500s. They were looking for **legendary** cities of gold. **Missionaries** came to spread Christianity, too.

Spain ruled this region until 1821. Then it became part of Mexico. It passed to the United States in 1848.

The White House Pueblo was built between 1060 and 1275 AD.

FORT BOWIE

Hike the trail to Fort Bowie, near Willcox. You'll pass an old stagecoach station. Then you'll pass an Apache wickiup, or dwelling. Finally, you reach the fort. There you'll see where soldiers ate and slept.

Many settlers moved into Arizona in the mid-1800s. They settled on land the Apaches owned. The Apaches tried to keep their land. They attacked ranches, forts, and towns. Fort Bowie's army troops fought them.

Cochise and Geronimo were Apache leaders. They kept on fighting. Cochise was forced to give up in 1872. The U.S. army promised Geronimo safety for his followers. So Geronimo gave up in 1886. Then he and his people were sent to Florida where they were jailed.

Wickiups were made with a wooden pole frame and covered with grass. This wickiup is near Fort Bowie.

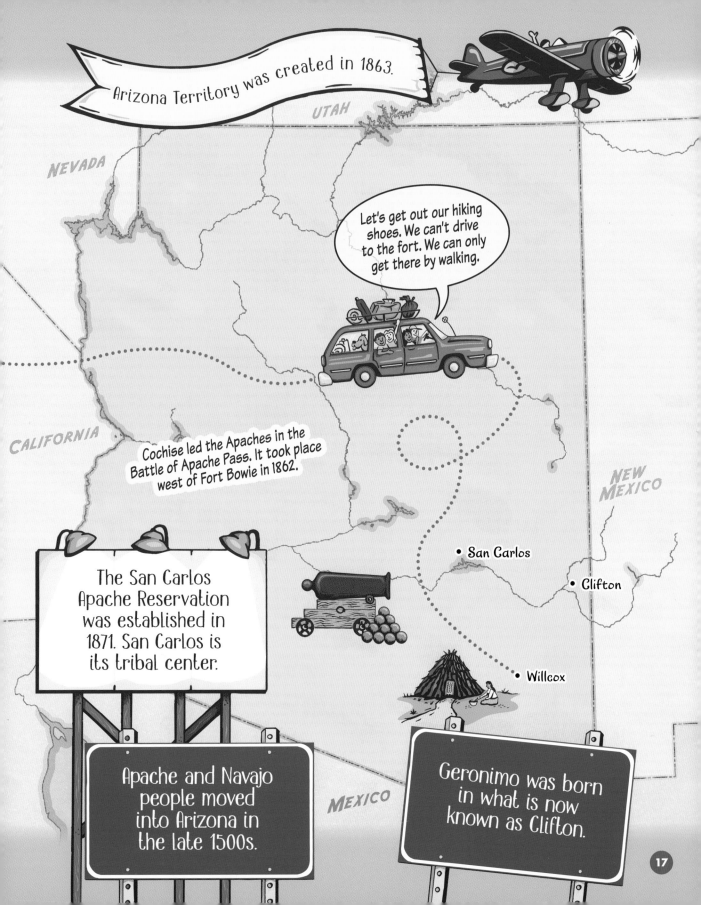

Arizona Territory was created in 1863.

UTAH

NEVADA

Let's get out our hiking shoes. We can't drive to the fort. We can only get there by walking.

CALIFORNIA

Cochise led the Apaches in the Battle of Apache Pass. It took place west of Fort Bowie in 1862.

NEW MEXICO

• San Carlos

• Clifton

The San Carlos Apache Reservation was established in 1871. San Carlos is its tribal center.

• Willcox

Apache and Navajo people moved into Arizona in the late 1500s.

MEXICO

Geronimo was born in what is now known as Clifton.

La Fiesta de Tumacácori takes place at Mission San José de Tumacácori, near Tubac. Father Eusebio Francisco Kino founded this mission in 1691.

About 30% of Arizonans are Hispanic.

UTAH

NEVADA

• Oraibi

• Window Rock

The Hopi village of Oraibi was founded in the 1100s.

NEW MEXICO

In 2016, 6,931,071 people lived in Arizona. It's the 14th-largest state by population.

Arizona has 22 Native American reservations. The largest is the Navajo reservation in northeast Arizona. Its capital is Window Rock.

The Hopi reservation is completely surrounded by the Navajo reservation. Most Hopi villages sit atop three **mesas**. They are called First Mesa, Second Mesa, and Third Mesa.

★ Phoenix   • Mesa

• Yuma

• Casa Grande

Tucson •

About 1 out of 20 Arizonans is Native American. Only California and Oklahoma have more Native Americans than Arizona.

Tubac •

MEXICO

POPULATION OF LARGEST CITIES
Phoenix................1,563,025
Tucson..................531,641
Mesa.....................471,825

18

Let's eat some tacos! Let's learn how to weave baskets! Let's listen to a storyteller!

LA FIESTA DE TUMACÁCORI

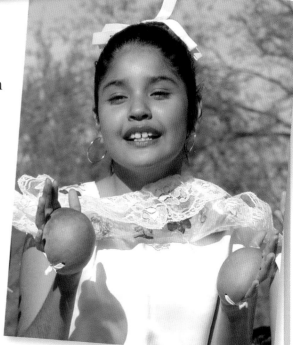

See a puppet show and swat a **piñata**. Watch Native American dancers and dashing horsemen. Taste loads of spicy, mouthwatering foods. You're at La Fiesta de Tumacácori! It celebrates Native American, **Hispanic**, and **Anglo** customs.

Many Arizona cities have Hispanic or Native American names. Casa Grande, Tucson, and Yuma are examples. Arizonans enjoy Mexican burritos and tamales. Fry bread, a traditional food for many Native American tribes including the Yaqui, is also popular in Arizona. Arizonans enjoy a great mix of cultures!

Thousands of people move to Arizona every year. They love the sunny climate. Arizona has grown since 1950. Almost nine times more people live there now!

Folklóricos, or Mexican folk dancers, perform at La Fiesta de Tumacácori.

GOLD RUSH DAYS IN WICKENBURG

Are you good at mucking? That means shoveling **ore** into a cart. Maybe you're good at panning for gold. You hold a pan in a running stream. If you're lucky, your pan might catch grains of gold!

You can enter contests for all these activities. Just drop by Wickenburg for Gold Rush Days! This festival celebrates an exciting time in history. Henry Wickenburg discovered gold in the area in 1863. Thousands of people swarmed in to get rich!

Both gold and silver were found in Arizona. But copper had long-lasting success. Copper-mining towns sprang up around Arizona. Now it's the top copper-mining state!

Visitors can pan for gold during Wickenburg's Gold Rush Days.

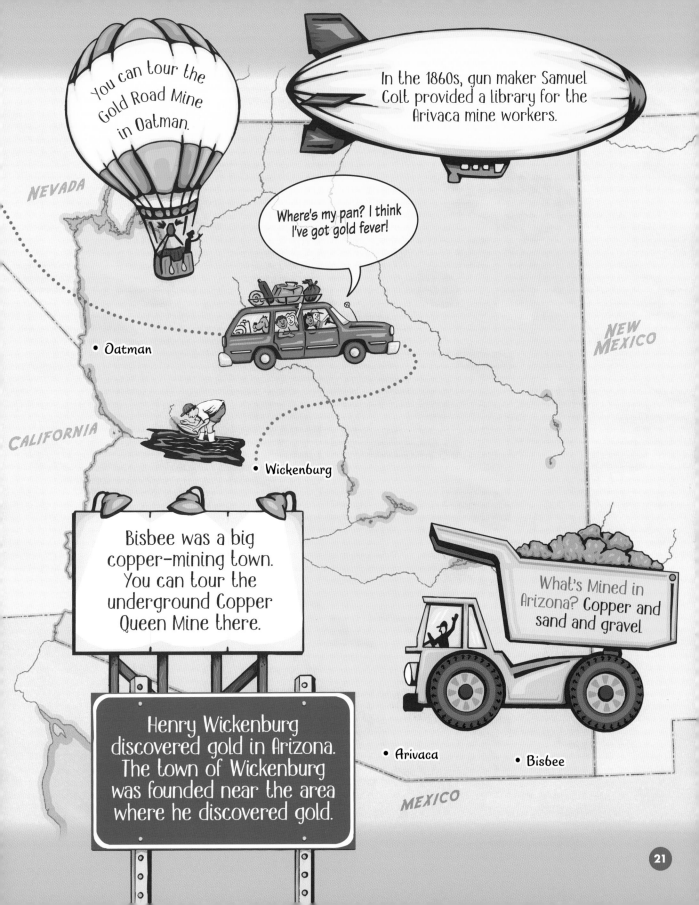

You can tour the Gold Road Mine in Oatman.

In the 1860s, gun maker Samuel Colt provided a library for the Arivaca mine workers.

NEVADA

Where's my pan? I think I've got gold fever!

• Oatman

NEW MEXICO

CALIFORNIA

• Wickenburg

Bisbee was a big copper-mining town. You can tour the underground Copper Queen Mine there.

What's Mined in Arizona? Copper and sand and gravel.

Henry Wickenburg discovered gold in Arizona. The town of Wickenburg was founded near the area where he discovered gold.

• Arivaca

• Bisbee

MEXICO

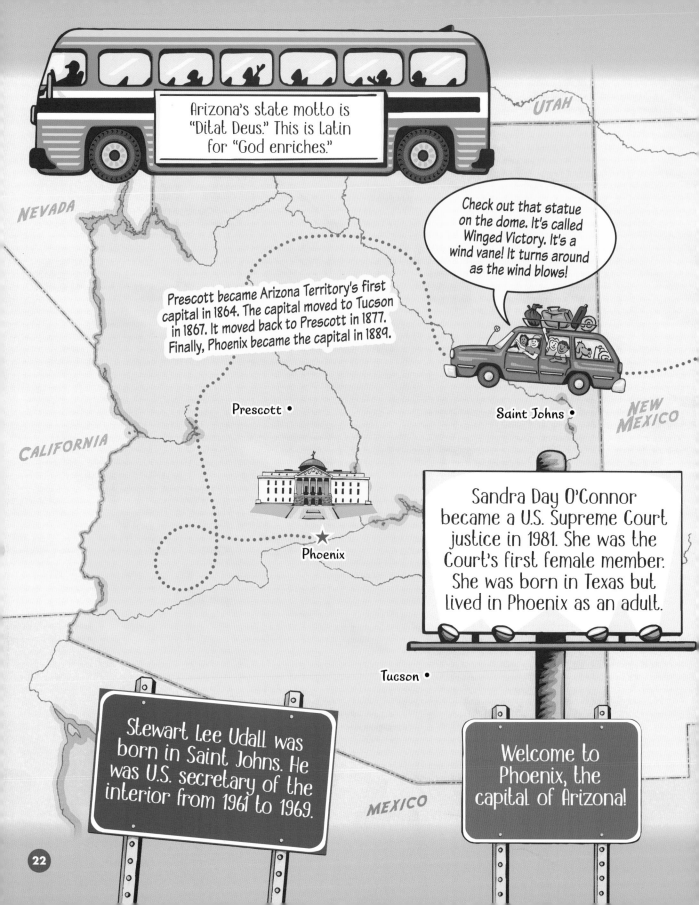

Arizona's state motto is "Ditat Deus." This is Latin for "God enriches."

Check out that statue on the dome. It's called Winged Victory. It's a wind vane! It turns around as the wind blows!

Prescott became Arizona Territory's first capital in 1864. The capital moved to Tucson in 1867. It moved back to Prescott in 1877. Finally, Phoenix became the capital in 1889.

Sandra Day O'Connor became a U.S. Supreme Court justice in 1981. She was the Court's first female member. She was born in Texas but lived in Phoenix as an adult.

Stewart Lee Udall was born in Saint Johns. He was U.S. secretary of the interior from 1961 to 1969.

Welcome to Phoenix, the capital of Arizona!

NEVADA

UTAH

CALIFORNIA

NEW MEXICO

Prescott •

Saint Johns •

★ Phoenix

Tucson •

MEXICO

THE STATE CAPITOL IN PHOENIX

Arizona mines lots of copper. Where does that copper go? All over the world. But some of it stays right at home. Just look at the state capitol. Its roof and dome are covered with copper!

This building is the center of state government. Arizona's government is organized like the U.S. government. It has three branches. One branch makes the state's laws. Another branch enforces the laws. That means it makes sure the laws are obeyed. The governor heads this branch. Judges make up the third branch. They listen to cases in court. Then they decide whether someone has broken a law.

The Arizona capitol also houses a museum. You can learn about the history of Arizona government.

TOMBSTONE AND THE O.K. CORRAL

The gunfighters look pretty mean. Suddenly, they draw their guns. *Bang, bang!* In a few puffs of smoke, it's over.

Don't worry. No one really gets shot. You're watching a show in Tombstone. People are acting out a famous scene. It's the gunfight at the O.K. Corral!

Tombstone was once a pretty wild town. Silver was discovered there in 1877. Thousands of people rushed in. They sometimes settled their quarrels with guns. That's what happened at the O.K. Corral in 1881.

Nine men took part in the historic gunfight. One famous gunman was Wyatt Earp. He is the subject of many movies and TV shows!

Actors recreate the gunfight at the O.K. Corral in Tombstone.

There's also a Boot Hill Cemetery outside of Dodge City, Kansas. Outlaws were buried there.

Oh, boy! We can take horse rides and stagecoach tours in Tombstone!

People who died in Tombstone were buried in Boothill Graveyard. You can visit the cemetery and look for famous names on the grave markers.

At the O.K. Corral, four men were on Wyatt Earp's side. They faced five men on Ike Clanton's side. Three members of Clanton's gang were killed.

Pioneer Living History Museum is in Phoenix. It's built like a town from Arizona Territory days.

The gunfight at the O.K. Corral took place on October 26, 1881.

NEVADA
UTAH
CALIFORNIA
NEW MEXICO
★ Phoenix
• Tombstone
MEXICO

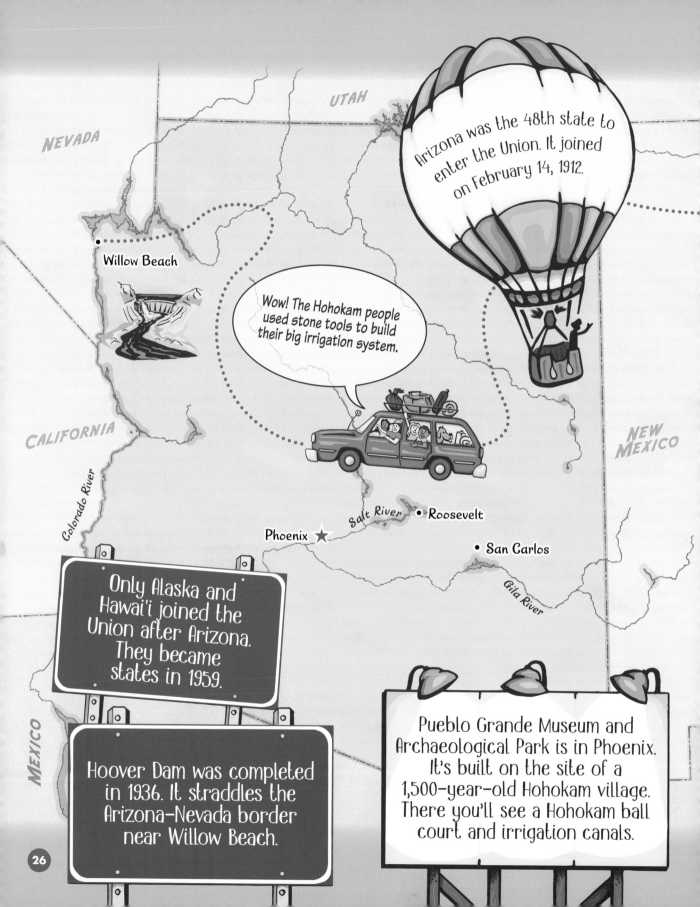

IRRIGATION AND THE HOOVER DAM

Arizona has big irrigation systems. They were created by building dams on rivers. Water builds up behind the dams. Then it's sent through irrigation **canals**. The dams create electricity with water power, too.

The Hoover Dam is one of the most famous dams. It is on the Colorado River. It provides water for many Arizona farms. It also makes hydroelectric power.

Arizona also built several dams on the Salt River. One was Roosevelt Dam, near Roosevelt. It opened in 1911. The Gila River's Coolidge Dam opened in 1928. It's near San Carlos.

The Hoover Dam's base is an impressive 660 feet (201 m) thick.

MORTIMER FARMS PUMPKIN FESTIVAL IN DEWEY-HUMBOLDT

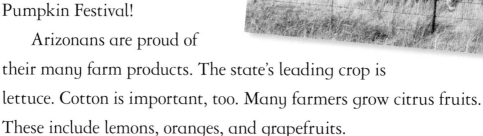

Ride a hay wagon around the farm. Solve the 10-acre (4 ha) corn maze. Then pick your own Halloween pumpkin. You're enjoying the Mortimer Farms Pumpkin Festival!

Arizonans are proud of their many farm products. The state's leading crop is lettuce. Cotton is important, too. Many farmers grow citrus fruits. These include lemons, oranges, and grapefruits.

Beef cattle graze on big ranches in Arizona. You'll see sheep nibbling the grasses, too. Is it springtime? Then you'll see new lambs prancing around!

Many cattle roam large pastures in Arizona.

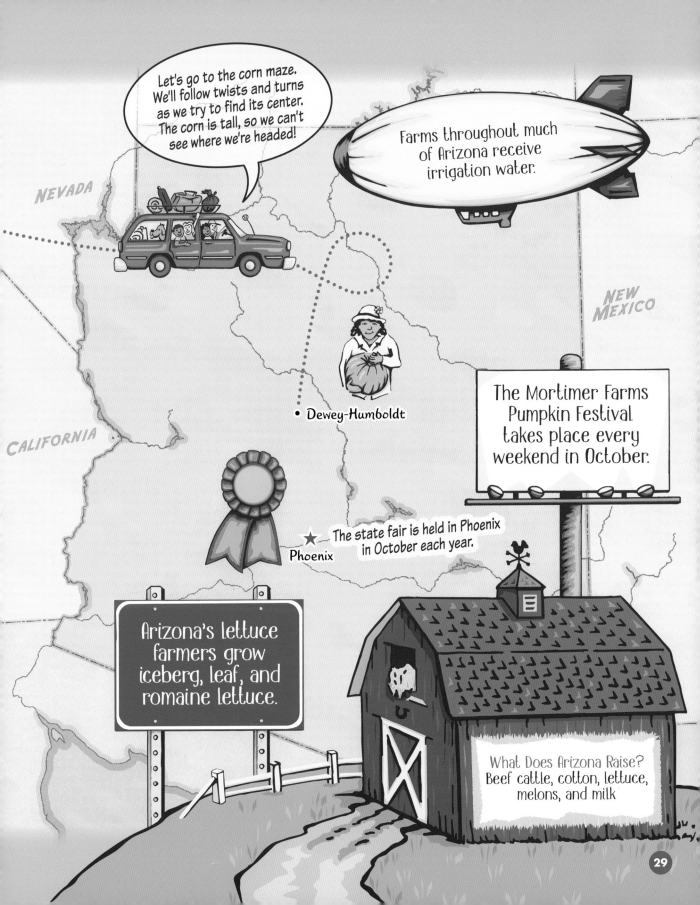

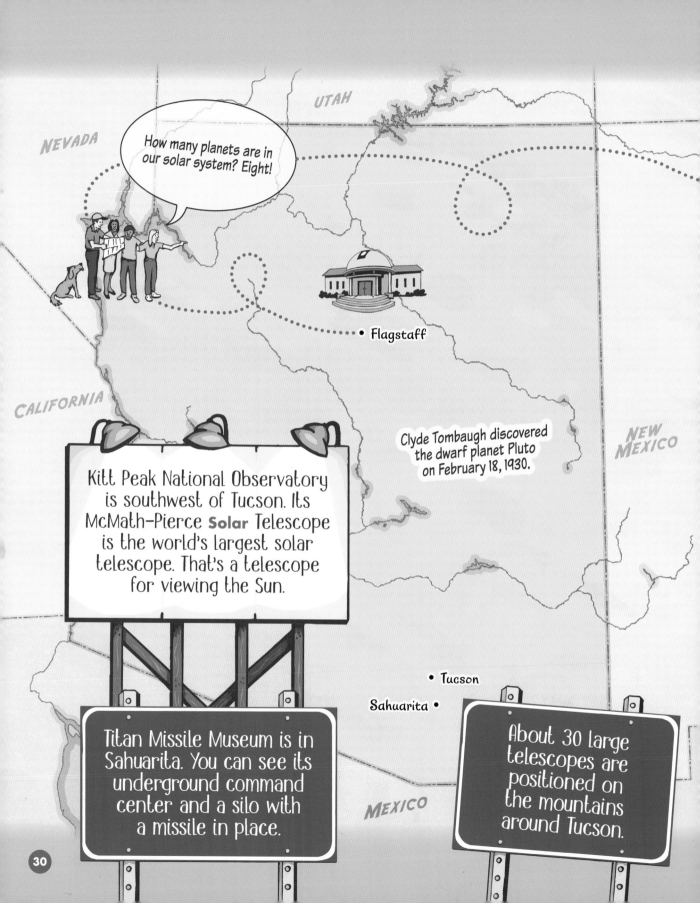

How many planets are in our solar system? Eight!

UTAH

NEVADA

CALIFORNIA

Flagstaff

Clyde Tombaugh discovered the dwarf planet Pluto on February 18, 1930.

NEW MEXICO

Kitt Peak National Observatory is southwest of Tucson. Its McMath-Pierce **Solar** Telescope is the world's largest solar telescope. That's a telescope for viewing the Sun.

Tucson

Sahuarita

Titan Missile Museum is in Sahuarita. You can see its underground command center and a silo with a missile in place.

About 30 large telescopes are positioned on the mountains around Tucson.

MEXICO

STARGAZING AT LOWELL OBSERVATORY

What does the Moon's surface look like? How about Saturn, Jupiter, and Mars? You'll see them all at Lowell Observatory in Flagstaff! Just take a nighttime tour. You can gaze through its massive telescope.

Arizona's clear skies come in handy. There is little moisture in the atmosphere to distort the view. Scientists can see objects in space clearly. An astronomer at Lowell Observatory found that out. He discovered the dwarf planet Pluto in 1930.

Clear skies are good for airplane pilots, too. This was helpful during World War II (1939–1945). Many military air bases opened in Arizona. After the war, Arizona's population soared. Thousands of people decided to settle there.

Astronomers have used the Clark Telescope at Lowell to study the stars since 1896.

THE PEANUT PATCH IN YUMA

Watch workers dump the peanuts into roasters. Then chomp on a warm, freshly roasted peanut. Next, watch machines grind the peanuts up. They might end up as peanut butter. Some peanuts go to the candy kitchen. They're made into peanut brittle and peanut fudge!

You're touring the Peanut Patch. This food factory makes delicious things with peanuts.

Arizona makes many food products. But computer equipment is the top factory item. Some factories make radios and TVs. Other factories make aircraft, spacecraft, missiles, or metals.

You can enjoy a variety of treats at the Peanut Patch!

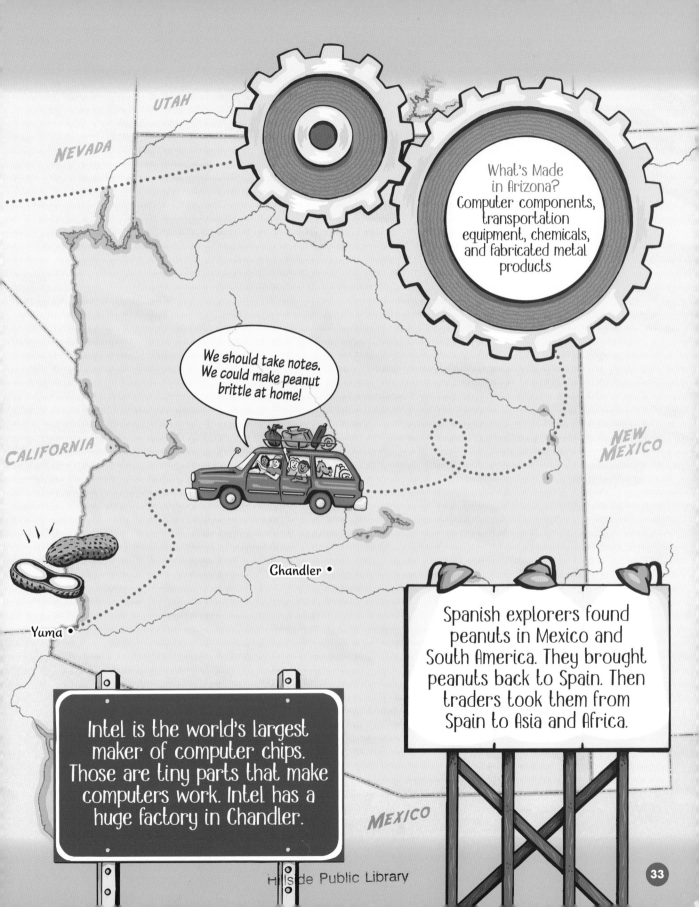

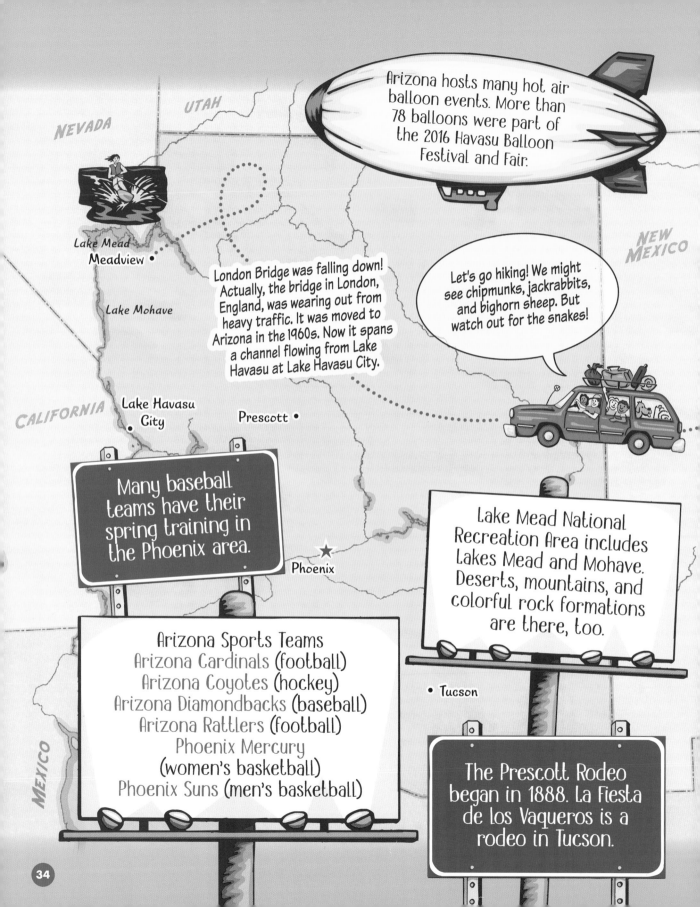

NEVADA

UTAH

Arizona hosts many hot air balloon events. More than 78 balloons were part of the 2016 Havasu Balloon Festival and Fair.

NEW MEXICO

Lake Mead
Meadview

London Bridge was falling down! Actually, the bridge in London, England, was wearing out from heavy traffic. It was moved to Arizona in the 1960s. Now it spans a channel flowing from Lake Havasu at Lake Havasu City.

Let's go hiking! We might see chipmunks, jackrabbits, and bighorn sheep. But watch out for the snakes!

Lake Mohave

CALIFORNIA

Lake Havasu City

Prescott

Many baseball teams have their spring training in the Phoenix area.

★ Phoenix

Lake Mead National Recreation Area includes Lakes Mead and Mohave. Deserts, mountains, and colorful rock formations are there, too.

Arizona Sports Teams
Arizona Cardinals (football)
Arizona Coyotes (hockey)
Arizona Diamondbacks (baseball)
Arizona Rattlers (football)
Phoenix Mercury
(women's basketball)
Phoenix Suns (men's basketball)

• Tucson

MEXICO

The Prescott Rodeo began in 1888. La Fiesta de los Vaqueros is a rodeo in Tucson.

FUN AT LAKE MEAD

You could spend weeks at Lake Mead! It's in Arizona's northwest corner, near Meadview. You can go boating, swimming, or fishing. Then you can explore the surrounding desert. Mountains and canyon walls rise in the distance.

Arizona's a great place for outdoor fun. In the winter, people come from cold states. They enjoy Arizona's warm weather. Meanwhile, skiers flock to the snowy mountains.

The Fiesta Bowl is an exciting sports festival. Fiesta Bowl events happen around New Year's Day. First, there's a big parade in Phoenix. Then college football champs play at University of Phoenix Stadium. Thousands of people join in the fun!

The land around Lake Mead has three of the four U.S. desert ecosystems: the Mojave, the Great Basin, and the Sonoran Deserts.

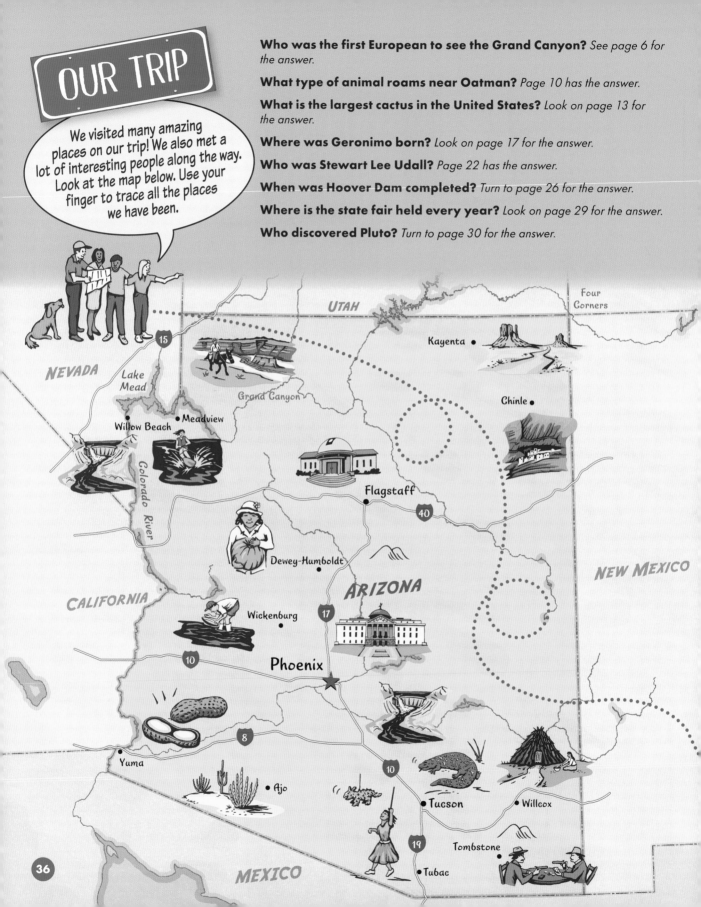

OUR TRIP

We visited many amazing places on our trip! We also met a lot of interesting people along the way. Look at the map below. Use your finger to trace all the places we have been.

Who was the first European to see the Grand Canyon? *See page 6 for the answer.*

What type of animal roams near Oatman? *Page 10 has the answer.*

What is the largest cactus in the United States? *Look on page 13 for the answer.*

Where was Geronimo born? *Look on page 17 for the answer.*

Who was Stewart Lee Udall? *Page 22 has the answer.*

When was Hoover Dam completed? *Turn to page 26 for the answer.*

Where is the state fair held every year? *Look on page 29 for the answer.*

Who discovered Pluto? *Turn to page 30 for the answer.*

UTAH

Four Corners

NEVADA

Lake Mead

Kayenta

Grand Canyon

Chinle

Willow Beach · Meadview

Colorado River

Flagstaff

40

Dewey-Humboldt

NEW MEXICO

ARIZONA

CALIFORNIA

Wickenburg

17

Phoenix

10

8

Yuma

Ajo

Tucson

Willcox

19

Tombstone

Tubac

MEXICO

STATE SYMBOLS

State amphibian: Arizona tree frog

State bird: Cactus wren

State butterfly: Two-tailed swallowtail

State fish: Apache trout

State flower: Saguaro cactus blossom

State fossil: Petrified wood

State gemstone: Turquoise

State mammal: Ringtail

State neckwear: Bola tie

State reptile: Arizona ridge-nosed rattlesnake

State tree: Palo verde

State seal

STATE SONG

"ARIZONA MARCH SONG"
Words by Margaret Rowe Clifford,
music by Maurice Blumenthal

Come to this land of sunshine
To this land where life is young.
Where the wide, wide world is
   waiting,
The songs that will now be sung.
Where the golden sun is flaming
Into warm, white shining day,
And the sons of men are blazing
Their priceless right of way.

Come stand beside the rivers
Within our valleys broad.
Stand here with heads
   uncovered,
In the presence of our God!
While all around, about us
The brave, unconquered band,
As guardians and landmarks
The giant mountains stand.

Not alone for gold and silver
Is Arizona great.
But with graves of heroes
   sleeping,
All the land is consecrate!
O, come and live beside us
However far ye roam
Come and help us build up
   temples
And name those temples "home."

Chorus:
Sing the song that's in your hearts
Sing of the great Southwest,
Thank God, for Arizona
In splendid sunshine dressed.
For thy beauty and thy grandeur,
For thy regal robes so sheen
We hail thee Arizona
Our Goddess and our queen.

That was a great trip! We have traveled all over Arizona! There are a few places that we didn't have time for, though. Next time, we plan to visit the Reid Park Zoo in Tucson. This zoo featured more than 450 animals in 2015.

State flag

FAMOUS PEOPLE

Aaron, Max (1992–), figure skater

Ali, Muhammad (1942–2016), boxer who lived in Arizona later in life

Apache Kid (ca. 1867–ca. 1910), Apache outlaw

Carbajal, Michael (1967–), boxer

Chávez, César (1927–1993), labor leader

Cochise (ca. 1812–1874), Apache leader

Espinoza, Louie (1962–), boxer

Fitzpatrick, Ryan (1982–), football player

Geronimo (1829–1909), Apache leader

Jonas, Joe (1989–), singer

Kino, Eusebio Francisco (1645–1711), mapmaker and missionary

Luke, Frank, Jr. (1897–1918), fighter pilot

McCain, John (1936–), politician

Nicks, Stevie (1948–), singer and songwriter

O'Connor, Sandra Day (1930–), Supreme Court justice

Poston, Charles (1825–1902), politician known as the Father of Arizona

Ronstadt, Linda (1946–), singer

Spade, David (1964–), comedian and actor

Stone, Emma (1988–), actor

Strug, Kerri (1977–), gymnast and Olympic medalist

Udall, Stewart Lee (1920–2010), politician

WORDS TO KNOW

ancestors (AN-sess-turz) a person's grandparents, great-grandparents, and so on

Anglo (ANG-low) descended from non-Hispanic European people

canals (kuh-NALZ) long ditches dug to create a waterway for travel or watering crops

culture (KUHL-chur) the beliefs, customs, and ways of life of a group of people

gorge (GORJ) a deep valley, often cut through rock by a river

Hispanic (hiss-PAN-ik) having roots in Spanish-speaking lands

irrigation (ihr-uh-GAY-shuhn) directing water from rivers or lakes into fields

legendary (LEJ-uhn-dair-ee) based on fantastic stories

mesas (MAY-suhz) steep-sided hills or mountains with flat tops

missionaries (MISH-uh-nair-eez) people who travel somewhere to spread their faith

ore (OR) rock that contains valuable minerals such as silver or gold

piñata (pin-YAH-tah) a decorated container filled with candy

plateaus (plah-TOZ) regions of high, level land

pueblo (PUEH-blow) a village

reservation (reh-zuhr-VAY-shuhn) land set aside by the U.S. government for Native Americans

solar (SO-lur) relating to the Sun

TO LEARN MORE

IN THE LIBRARY

Bauer, Marion Dane. *Celebrating Arizona.* Boston, MA: Houghton Mifflin Harcourt, 2013.

Chin, Jason. *Grand Canyon.* New York, NY: Roaring Brook Press, 2017.

Friedman, Mark. *The Apache.* New York, NY: Children's Press, 2011.

Turner, Jim. *Arizona: A Celebration of the Grand Canyon State.* Layton, UT: Gibbs Smith, 2011.

ON THE WEB

Visit our Web site for links about Arizona:
childsworld.com/links

Note to Parents, Teachers, and Librarians: We routinely verify our Web links to make sure they are safe and active sites. So encourage your readers to check them out!

PLACES TO VISIT OR CONTACT

Arizona History Museum
arizonahistoricalsociety.org/tucson
949 East Second Street
Tucson, AZ 85719
502/628-5774
For more information about the history of Arizona

Arizona Office of Tourism
tourism.az.gov
118 N. 7th Avenue, Suite 400
Phoenix, AZ 85007
602/364-3700
For more information about traveling in Arizona

Arizona covers 113,998 square miles (295,253 sq km). It's the 6th-largest state in size.

INDEX

Bye, Grand Canyon State. We had a great time. We'll come back soon!